Phil H. LISTEMANN

Colour profiles: Gaetan Marie/Bravo Bravo Aviation

Layout & project design: Phil Listemann

Copyright © Phil Listemann 2014
updated June 2019, revised February 2021

ISBN 978-2918590-35-4

Edited by Phil H. Listemann

www.RAF-IN-COMBAT.com

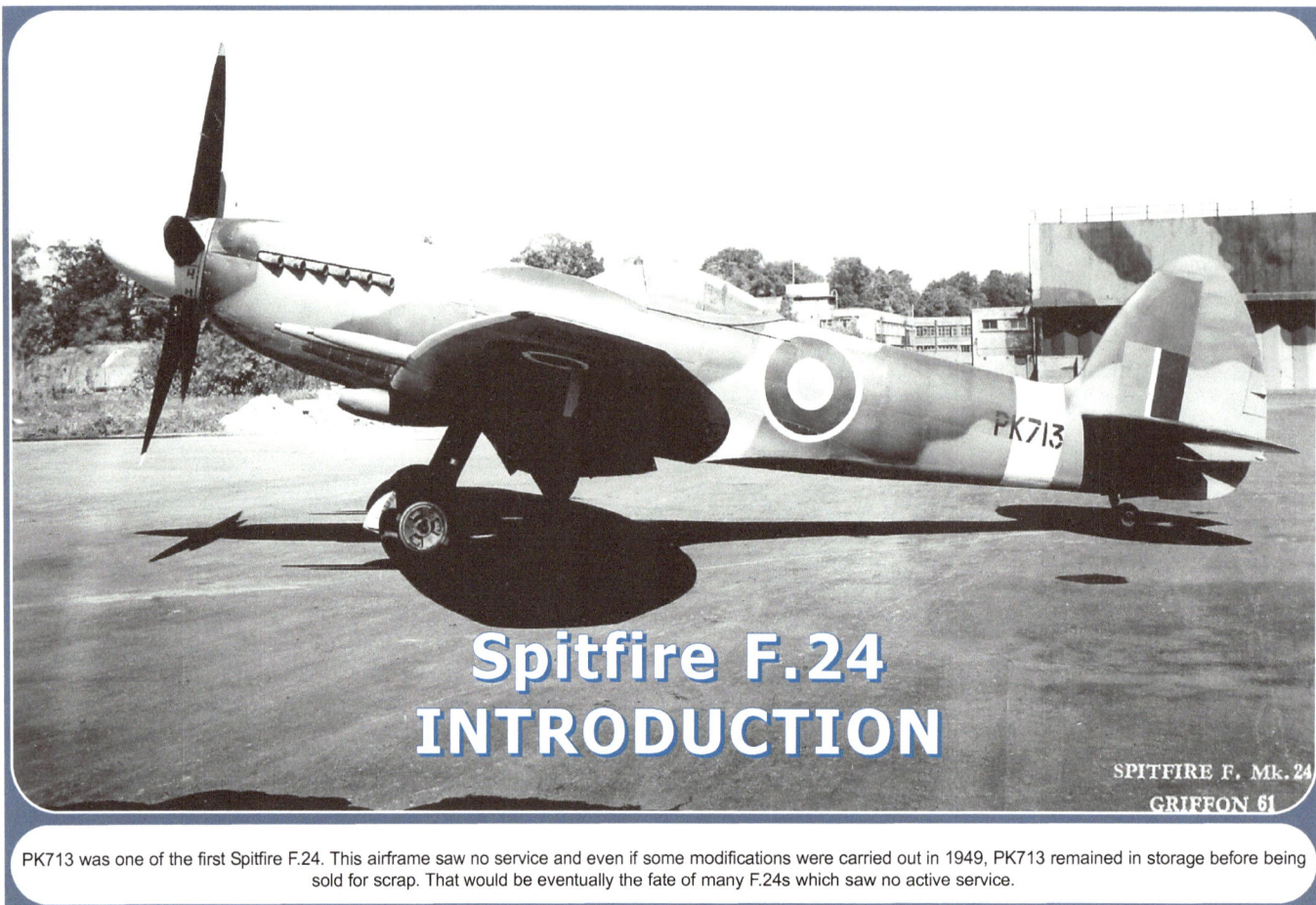

Spitfire F.24
INTRODUCTION

SPITFIRE F. Mk. 24
GRIFFON 61

PK713 was one of the first Spitfire F.24. This airframe saw no service and even if some modifications were carried out in 1949, PK713 remained in storage before being sold for scrap. That would be eventually the fate of many F.24s which saw no active service.

The Spitfire F.24 was the ultimate version of the legendary fighter that had been developed continuously since the prototype first flew in 1936. There were only eight years between the two marks, but so many improvements and modifications! The F.24 was basically an improved version of the F.22, which was itself an improved version of the F.21. With the F.21, the RAF had introduced its third and last generation of Spitfire with significant changes to the airframe. The F.22 was, simply, the teardrop canopy, low back version of the F.21. The F.24, in turn, incorporated modifications such as wing-pickup points for zero-length rocket launchers and the fitting of two additional fuel tanks in the rear fuselage. An electrical gun-firing system replaced the pneumatic system used on the F.22. The cannons installed were also the last of their type (short barrel 20mm Hispano Mk.Vs). Some early F.24s were modified and fitted with the long-barrel version as carried by the F.22. All of these improvements were, really, insignificant and, at the time, it was even thought a new denomination was not justified as a different mark of engine was not installed. Supermarine referred to them initially as F.22s, but the RAF applied the correct designation.

The prototype of the F.24 was former Spitfire F.22 PK313 which made its first flight as an F.24 on 27 February 1946. The F.24 was built in small numbers – just 85, including seven conversions from F.22s (**PK313**, **PK515**, **PK627**, **PK677**, **PK680**, **PK684**, **PK715**). They were delivered between August 1946 and February 1948 – 60 in 1946, 21 in 1947 and four in 1948. The first 27 built were diverted from a current F.22 order. The serials allocated were therefore **PK678**, **PK679**, **PK681-683**, **PK685-689**, **PK712-714**, and **PK716-726**. The remaining 54 aircraft were built from a reduced order for 150 F.24s (but recor-

ded as F.22s by Supermarine), ordered in November 1945, and the serials allocated were **VN301-348** and **VN477-496**. At the time of the F.24's introduction to service, jet-powered aircraft were already seen as the way of the future. Every fighter pilot wanted to fly a jet, not a Spitfire. However, in this age of transition, modern air forces saw the need for prop-driven aircraft for ground attack duties as the Korean War would soon prove. Jets were not yet totally suited for ground attack roles as they were, at that time, too vulnerable to ground fire. The problem for the British, however, was that they didn't have enough money to buy both types so the potent F.24 was overlooked as priority was given to the production of jet aircraft.

A deep look at the career of each F.24 reveals a surprising one-third were stored, and never used by any flying unit, and none were exported like earlier marks of Spitfire. The F.24 got its chance, however, when the RAF chose it when reinforcements were needed in the Far East (Hong Kong in particular). That meant the RAF still believed in the capabilities of the Spitfire as an effective fighting aircraft. Tensions increased when, in 1949, Mao was about to take power of continental China. This was followed by the intervention of the Chinese in Korea the following year (where British troops were fighting under the UN banner). That made a full-blown conflict with Communist China highly probable if things turned for the worse. The Spitfire F.24 was seen as a major asset in the region and would have probably proven it was superior to the Mustang then engaged in Korea. History was not written that way though. Ironically, the last RAF operational Spitfire flight was highly publicised, but it was by a reconnaissance variant. The last flight of the last fighter variant (the role that made the legend), the F.24, was much less publicised!

A three-fourth view from behind of PK713 showing the impressive tail which was designed and introduced with the F.22. It is not always easy to identify a F.24 from a F.22, and this picture is confirming that fact once more.

TECHNICAL DATA
SPITFIRE F.24

Manufacturer:
Vickers-Armstrong (Castle Bromwich)

Type :
fighter-bomber

Accommodation:
One pilot

Power plant:
One 1,540 hp Rolls-Royce Griffon 61 or 64

Fuel & Oil
Fuel (Imp Gal):

186 [845.5 l]
(plus one possible 90 - 409 l - auxiliary drop tank)

Oil (Imp Gal):
9 [40.9 l]

Dimensions:
Span : 36 ft 11 in [11,25 m]
Length : 32 ft 11 in [9,91 m]
Height : 13 ft 6 in [4,12 m]

Weights:
Empty : 7,351 lb [3 341 kg]
Gross : 10,150 lb [4 614 kg]

Performance :
Max speed : 454 mph at 26,000 ft
[731 km/h at 7 900 m]
Rate of climb : 4,900ft/min [124m/min]
Service ceiling : 43,000 ft [13 000 m]

Armament :
4 x Hispano 20mm Mk.II (or Mk.V) cannons with 175rpd (inboard) and 150rpg (outboard).
Provision for one 500-lb (227 kg) under each wing and under the fuselage, or rockerts of 3-in.

Impressive view of PK713 with the five-blade propeller and the four 20mm cannons. At first the Spitfire F.24 did not have any rack to carry rockets. Racks were installed later on making the F.24 as a potent fighter-bomber but this was never proved in combat. *(Peter Arnold col.)*

THE UNITS

Photo of poor quality but seeing some Spitfire F.24s flying in formation is rare. This photo highlights the various markings the F.24s had worn while in service in Hong Kong, with a mixture of roundels - pre and post 1947 -, lack of camouflage for an handful of aircraft and even the squadron's codes are not painted in the same order! . Note the spinner, either painted partially in red (for W2-D in the front), either in blue for all the other four. Silver finish seems to have appeared by the end of its service life in the Far East. *(via Andrew Thomas)*

No.80 Squadron
code : W2
January 1948 - January 1952

Only one RAF squadron was equipped with the Spitfire F.24. No.80 Squadron, previously a Tempest unit, was based in Germany and commanded by S/L Richard A. Newberry. He was awarded the DFC and Bar while flying with No. 118 Squadron during the war. Another DFC recipient was serving with the squadron, F/L Frank G. Fray, a former reconnaissance pilot during the war, commanded A Flight. On 15 January, 1948, the first four F.24s were collected from Lyneham (VN301, VN308, VN310 and VN311) and flown to Manston but due to bad weather the trip to Germany could not be made before the 22nd when S/L Newberry, F/O Colvin and P/O Coop finally arrived at Wunstorff. F/O Clark, piloting one of the Spitfires, was obliged to stay at Manston because his aircraft had become unserviceable. These first three Spitfires were immediately put to good use and used to convert several of the squadron's pilots. On 7 February two more Spitfires (PK678 and VN315) arrived and with other arrivals 80 Sqn could count on 11 F.24s by the 18th (VN304, VN312, VN319, VN322, VN323) with two more added on the 20th (VN303, VN307). Conversion training continued during the month with familiarisation flights, formation pairs, aerobatics and climbs to height becoming the routine. By the end of the month about 70 hours' flying had been completed. Initial poor serviceability soon improved once the ground crews

became used to the new type. Ice and snow prevented any flying in early March and this did not resume until the 10th. On the 15th six F.24s provided escort as far as the Dutch frontier to Lord Tedder, the Chief of Air Staff, who had visited the station. Otherwise training continued normally with good weather until the 25th when flying ceased in order to prepare for a month's detachment to APC Lubeck in April. In all the squadron logged 100 hours during March.

Over the next few months the Squadron continued its routine flights and logged between 100 and 150 hours per month up to October. That month 164 sorties were carried out and close to 190 hours flown but a tragic accident occurred on the 28th. While leading a formation of six aircraft the CO's Spitfire (VN319) was struck from below and behind by his number five (F/L Hall in VN323) and both pilots were forced to abandon their aircraft. However the parachute of the CO opened before he left the cockpit entirely and he was fatally injured. Hall landed on the ground safely. Fray took over the command of the squadron pending the arrival of a new CO, S/L Eric W. Tremlett DFC, who had fought in the Far East with No. 20 Squadron. By the end of 1948 the squadron was maintaining a good level of serviceability and an average of 250 hours was flown in both November and December.

In 1949 routine flights continued with an average of 200 hours being allocated to the squadron to maintain a good level of skills. The typical types of flight were normally divided between formations (40 hours), tactical exercises (36 hours), cine came-

5

ra work (12 hours), navigation (22 hours) and armament training (rocket projectile practice and low level bombing). The remaining 50 or so hours were used for other tasks like first solo for new comers and other training exercises like GCA or interceptions. In all the average of number of hours flown by each pilot per month was around 18 (in other words more or less half an hour per day). Accidents were unavoidable and on 7 March P/O Ronald A. Clements was killed in VN306 during a formation flight. It is believed he partially lost vision while pulling out after a dive. VN306 struck the ground and severely injured the pilot who died later in hospital. In May economic restrictions were lifted as the Squadron was planning to convert to the Vampire so there was no reason to preserve the Spitfire F.24s as the end of their careers had been decided. Close to 300 hours were logged on Spitfires that month and the pilots could fly much more as usual. Their plans changed totally when, on the 31st, the personnel were informed that, instead of receiving new aircraft, they were going to be sent to the Far East instead! This change had been decided because of the situation in China, the takeover by the Communist forces now being seen as inevitable, exposing Hong Kong as nothing was really known about Chinese intentions regarding the British colony. Consequently reinforcements were needed to at least demonstrate to the Chinese that the Crown was ready to defend Hong Kong. The Spitfire F.24 was the best aerial asset suitable for the facilities at Kai Tak where other Spitfire marks, FR.18s and PR.19s, were also stationed.

Because of this impending move the personnel became very busy and little time was reserved for flying duties so, consequently, the number of hours completed in June dropped to 60. Indeed, inspections had to be carried out on all aircraft, which needed time, and many of the F.24s were grounded as a result. The results of these inspections led to the decision to replace four of the F.24s on strength and eventually the replacement aircraft (PK712, PK723, VN488 and VN493) were issued to the squadron on 15 August. In the meantime the squadron was ready to be shipped out by sea. All of the equipment had been crated and on the 27th three Dakotas were made available to ferry the ground stores to the UK while the aircraft were flown to Renfrew in Scotland where they were to be put on board an aircraft carrier. On the ferry flight, the CO - S/L Tremlett - wrecked his Spitfre on landing at Renfrew on 2 July 1949.

The squadron, and the aircraft on board HMS *Ocean*, arrived at Hong Kong on 17th August. Most of August was spent unloading equipment, of course, and moving into the new quarters. Flying resumed on 20 August, even though the squadron was not yet fully operational, and familiarisation flights and local recce flights were first carried out. Sadly, things started badly for the squadron in the region when, on the 23rd, a tragic event occurred. F/O William R. Pickering was killed during his first solo from Kai Tak. Despite being briefed to make one dummy approach, overshoot and land on the second the pilot attempted to land off the first approach but was out of position and tightened his final turn to regain the runway heading. The Spitfire (PK723) stalled at low altitude and dived into the ground leaving no chance of survival for the pilot. Landing at Kai Tak was a challenge for the pilots unfamiliar with the area and another accident occurred six days later but, fortunately, without major consequences for the pilot. F/L Hall overshot the runway while retracting his undercarriage at the same time. The F.24 (VN488) suffered considerable damage and never flew again after having been inspected and becoming a spare parts source for the remaining Spitfires of the squadron. It was finally SOC two years later.

In September the squadron became fully operational in the area even though the absence of a firing range prevented any armament training. Two hundred and thirty-nine hours were logged that month (the squadron was allocated 300) with only formation and practice armed reconnaissance flights over the New Territories being carried out. This number of hours was seen as being satisfactory especially as a typhoon had passed not very far from Hong Kong early in the month and no flights were flown

Upon arrival in Hong Kong harbour, No.80 Sqn Spitfires F.24s were craned from the carrier HMS *Ocean* on to a lighter transfer ashore.

No.80 Squadron's Spitfire F.24s at Kai Tak airfield with the mountainous terrain around the colony. This photo was taken in November 1949 and W2-B was still wearing the pre-1947 roundels. Note the extra belly fuel tank on the ground close to a ground-crewman.

Spitfire F.24 VN489/W2-A was normally the CO's mount - S/L Tremlett - by January 1950. This airframe saw its markings evolve over the months but was particular as having a mixture of roundels, the pre-1947 roundel without the yellow outlined ring. Seems that the Squadron Leader pennant is absent here, but was later added. *(via Andrew Thomas)*

during this time. The monthly target of 300 hours was actually reached in October - Communist China was officially proclaimed on the 1st - and many exercises were performed with the Army. Now, as the Communists were the masters of continental China, the danger had become real and grown closer day by day as still nothing was really known about Mao's intentions for the New Territories. On the other side the Nationalists were retreating to Formosa and, on three occasions, Chinese Nationalist Mitchells (or believed to be) were seen flying along the borders and their intentions not clearly identified. No incursions were officially reported and the Mitchells certainly did not show hostile intent towards the British as they were fully occupied evacuating troops to the island that would become Taiwan. On the last day of October the squadron received instructions to have two fully-armed F.24s at readiness from dawn to dusk just in case.

Spitfire F.24 W2-U seen at Sek Kong. Most Squadron's Mk.24 had a simplified squadron badge painted on the tail. Note the white and black bands painted on the fuselage and wings. They were introduced after the Korean War had begun in case of the 80 had to be sent there on a short notice under the UN banner, but this never happened. Unfortunately these bands are hiding the serial, only the letters 'PK' are visible.

In November the Squadron had to face a maintenance problem as all of the F.24s were due to be inspected at the same time! To minimise the interruption to normal flying duties it was decided to reduce the number of hours for the month to allow the mechanics to get the job done. The pilots, despite the reduced hours, flew some air exercises with the Fireflies of the FAA (the Royal Navy having a fleet in the region - HMS *Triumph* and HMS *Unicorn* - to demonstrate once more the will to defend Hong Kong). Training with the aircraft of the FAA continued in December despite the fact that the Spitfire F.24s were ready to leave Hong Kong for Butterworth in Malaya in case of a violent reaction from the Nationalists when the Communist government in Peking was recognised by the British government (something which officially occurred on 7 January 1949). The move could not be done because of the bad weather and training resumed on the 13th - not for the good, however, as three minor accidents occurred that day. The worst was yet to come as on the 28th F/O Kenneth R. Rosewell, while being engaged in a cine gun exercise, called his wingman, Pilot II Williams, to report the engine of his Spitfire (VN305) had cut and that he was bailing out. He did so but was posted missing and, despite intensive searches in the next following days, was never found.

Standing patrols of two hours' duration with armed aircraft were maintained in January (4th to 8th and the 9th until midday) all day long from the new airstrip of Set Kong. The Spitfire F.24s were sometimes vectored to a Nationalist Commando or Dakota flying close to the British Colony but none crossed the boundaries. In addition to patrols two aircraft were kept at immediate cockpit readiness with four more at 30 minutes' readiness. On the 12th the squadron returned to Kai Tak. Routine tasks became the norm from that point with 300 hours allocated each month and patrol duty shared with No. 28 Squadron flying

Spitfire FR.18s. However 80 Squadron had to report the loss of one pilot and aircraft on 27 February (PK716) when Pilot III Lewis V. Firmin struck the sea while carrying out a practice attack. The Spitfire disintegrated on hitting the water and he was killed instantly. In March routine flying continued until the 7th when the F.24s were scrambled twice without results. During the month only 220 hours were logged mainly due to bad weather which had prevented any flying over the region for a couple of days. April was better with 266 hours flown. The target of 300 hours for the month could not be reached because of the Easter break and bad weather. Eleven and a half days were unfit for flying because stratus cloud at 800 feet frequently disturbed the normal training operations. The next two months were uneventful and even the deterioration of the situation in Korea after 25 June didn't change anything for the daily taskings. July continued in this vein but on the 26th the squadron lost another pilot, F/L Archibald P. Clark, when his Spitfire (VN491) entered a spin from which he did not recover. The aircraft was seen hitting the sea near Ninepin Island. By that time the number of hours allocated had been increased to 350. This target was surpassed in August with 366 hours flown but for the other months this figure could not be reached (remaining around 260-280 hours). The situation remained unchanged until the end of the year.

In January 1951 the squadron flew more than 400 sorties representing 367 hours flying. However the unit had to record another loss. F/L Denis F. White was killed while flying in formation in cloud. He was seen to go into a climb and White reported that his instruments had toppled. He ditched off Hong Kong. Despite intensive searches no trace was found of either the pilot or aircraft. Denis White was a very experienced pilot who had fought in Italy during the war with 241 Sqn and had earned the DFC. In February, due to bad weather, the number of sorties and hours flown dropped down to 288 and 231 respectively. March was not better (257/238) but conditions improved in April (243/293). In May the figures rose to 368 and 351 and the squadron was involved in a major exercise with other units (ground and air) with the F.24s loaded with operational armaments. On the 24th S/L Tremlett, tour-expired, left the squadron for England. Command was given to F/L Laughton pending the arrival of the new Commanding Officer. In June the Squadron could not reach its required number of hours (249) but did considerably better in July (304) while still waiting for the new CO. During those two months many exercises were carried out in conjunction with the Navy or other squadrons like No. 88 Squadron with its Sunderlands. The new CO, S/L John M.V. Carpenter, eventually arrived at the squadron on the 9th. He was an experienced pilot with a DFC and Bar on his chest - both awards received while fighting over Malta and the Mediterranean during the war. Otherwise August remained uneventful with 217 hours flown in 225 sorties. In September the squadron was handicapped with a shortage of aircraft and pilots that partially explained the low number of sorties performed that month (234/207). The other reason was also the passage of two typhoons that ran through the area. Until the end of the year nothing special was reported. Another 665 flight hours were achieved with 136 of those in December. The small number of hours flown in December was due to the fact that conversion from the Spitfire F.24 to the Hornet F.3 had begun and flying on the Spitfire stopped. On the 22nd a last formation of Spitfires was put up for photographing and posterity and marked the end of the Spitfire F.24's career in the RAF.

If we except the handful of machines used for various, trials the Spitfire F.24 hasn't been used by any units other than 80 Sqn. Most of the aircraft remained in storage during their whole time under RAF charge. However several aircraft were given a second chance when transferred to the newly formed Hong Kong Auxiliary Air Force and Malayan Auxiliary Air Force. For the Malayan Aux.AF, only three F.24 coming from FEAF stocks were taken on charge (PK681, PK683 and VN494) but little is known about their career which was short anyway. The HKAAF, formed on 1 May 1949 it received the prefix 'Royal' in 1951 – RHKAAF. From this first 1949 incarnation emerged the Hong Kong Auxiliary Squadron on 1 October 1950. Harvards formed the majority of the unit's strength but a couple of Spitfire FR.18s and PR.19s (formerly 28 Sqn and 81 Sqn respectively that had been based at Hong Kong) were also on hand. Eight Spitfire F.24s were added to the inventory (PK687, PK719, PK720, VN308, VN313, VN318, VN485 and VN492) in April and May 1952 and provided a significant boost to the combat capabilities of the RHKAAF. The arrival of the F.24 led to the withdrawal of the FR.18 in November 1952.

The RHKAAF used the Spitfire F.24 until it was withdrawn from use in early 1955. Several accidents occurred during those three years including one that caused the death of the CO, S/L Eric Gauntlett. On 12 June, 1954, while engaged in a practice attack on a ground target, the aircraft pulled up sharply and the engine failed. It was seen to pick up but items appeared to fall from the aircraft and it was seen to stall and dive vertically into the sea leaving no chance for the pilot to survive. In previous months three other F.24s had been lost: PK720 on 16 August, 1953, after an engine failure, ditched just off Kai Tak and ended up upside down in shallow water. The pilot, F/O H.L. Mose, was lucky enough to escape with no major injuries from this experience! Then, less than two months later, on 3 October 1953, VN313 and VN492 were lost. The first swung on landing. Its port wing hit a building and its undercarriage collapsed. The pilot, P/O George Bain escaped unhurt. VN492 was also lost in a landing incident just prior to VN313. The aircraft, flown by P/O R. Heard, turned onto the grass at the end of its landing run and tipped up. The damage was actually superficial but an airman shinned up the fuselage and pulled the tail down with such force that the skin was wrinkled.

With the loss of S/L Gauntlett the Squadron could count on only two Spitfire F.24s - VN318 and VN485 - as PK687 and VN308 were both struck off charge in December 1953. They were due for overhaul but this was seen as a waste of time so they helped in providing spare parts. The two remaining flying Spitfires soldiered on until being withdrawn in April 1955. This was the definitive end of the service flying career of the ultimate version of the Spitfire.

PK313
Built as F.22. Vickers-Armstrong 18.09.46 for conversion as F.24 to become the prototype of the mark; 9 MU 04.11.49; 29 MU 09.01.1950; NES 20.04.54. Sold for scrap 30.10.56.

PK515
Built as F.22. Vickers-Armstrong 29.11.46 for conversion as F.24; 33 MU 03.03.47; Westland 10.03.49 for mods; NEA 14.12.54. Sold for scrap 13.03.56.

PK627
Built as F.22. 33 MU 11.02.46; Vickers-Armstrong 15.05.46 for conversion as F.24; 32 MU 28.01.47; Westland 30.03.49 for mods; NES 14.12.54. Sold for scrap 28.06.56.

PK677
Built as F.22. 29 MU 11.02.46; Vickers-Armstrong 10.05.46 for conversion as F.24; 32 MU 28.01.47; Westland 01.02.49 for mods; NEA 04.12.54. Sold for scrap 02.11.56.

PK678
First flight 27.02.46; 6 MU 29.11.46; **80 Sqn** as 06.02.48; NES 16.06.53 sold for scrap 24.05.54.

PK679
First flight 08.03.46; 33 MU 25.10.46; Westland 28.03.49 for mods; NEA 14.12.54 sold for scrap 13.06.56.

PK680
Buit as F.22. 33 MU 11.02.46; Vickers-Armstrong 31.10.46 for conversion as F.24; 33 MU 28.01.47; Westland 07.03.49 for mods. NEA 14.12.54. Sold for scrap 17.05.56.

PK681
First flight 08.03.46; 33 MU 28.11.46 RNAS Renfrew 29.06.49; Seletar Singapore 12.08.49; Maintenance Base FE 11.09.50; Singapore AAF 20.07.51; 390 MU 07.03.52. SOC 15.04.54.

PK682
First flight 19.02.46; 33 MU 13.08.46; 1BR&SD 22.09.48; **80 Sqn** 29.09.48 FEAF. SOC 28.08.51.

PK683
First flight 19.02.46; 33 MU 13.08.46; Pyrrhus 12.08.50; FEAF 07.09.50; Maintenance Base FE storage 12.09.50; Singapore AAF 24.07.51; Hit PK681 while taxying at Tengah 29.09.52; Not repaired; 390MU 10.02.53. SOC 15.04.54. Became intructional airframe as 7150M. Extant Hall of Aviation Southampton.

PK684
Built as F.22. Vickers-Armstrong 11.02.46 for conversion as F.24. 33 MU 28.01.47; Westland 09.03.49 for mods. NEA 14.12.54. Sold for scrap 17.05.56.

PK685
First flight 27.02.46; 33 MU 13.09.46; Westland 03.02.49 for mods; NEA 14.12.54. Sold for scrap 13.06.56.

PK686
First flight 27.02.46; 33 MU 30.10.46; Westland 18.01.49 for mods NEA 14.12.54. Sold for scrap 28.06.56.

PK687
First flight 06.03.46; 33 MU 18.10.46; FEAF 28.03.50; Maintenance Base FE storage 18.05.50; Station HQ Kai Tak 03.10.50; **80 Sqn** 05.09.51; HKAAF 15.05.52. SOC 11.12.53.

PK688
First flight 19.02.46; 33 MU 30.10.46; Westland 12.04.49 for mods; NEA 14.12.54. Sold for scrap 17.02.56.

Above: Spitfire F.24 PK682 in flight over the British Colony. Note the fin flash of post-1947 style and the WW2 roundel on the fuselage.

below, PK719 of HKAAF taken while taxiing on the taxiway at Set Kong airfield. Its individual letter is believed to be 'Q'.

Spitfire F.24 VN304, W2-R, during a military ceremony at Lübeck in April 1948. Sent in the Far East with No.80 Sqn, it was eventually struck off charge in October 1950.
(Andrew Thomas)

PK689
First flight 27.02.46; 33 MU 27.09.46; Westland 07.01.49 for mods; HQ BAFO ComSqn 08.08.51; NEA 14.12.54. Sold for scrap 28.06.56.

PK712
First flight 06.03.46; 33 MU 26.11.46; RNAS Renfrew 04.07.48; **80 Sqn** FEAF 15.08.48; 390 MU 01.03.52. SOC 01.07.53.

PK713
First flight 19.02.46; 33 MU 11.09.46; Westland 04.02.49 for mods; NEA 14.12.54. Sold for scrap 02.11.56.

PK714
First flight 08.03.46; 33 MU 11.11.46; Westland 24.01.49 for mods; NEA 14.12.54. Sold for scrap 02.11.56.

PK715
Built as F.22. 29 MU 11.02.46; Vickers-Armstrong 16.05.46 for conversionas F.24; 33 MU 28.01.47; Westland 29.03.49 for mods. NEA 14.12.54. Sold for scrap 17.02.56.

PK716
33 MU 30.09.46; RNAS Renfrew 04.07.49; Seletar 02.08.49; **80 Sqn** 05.09.49; On 27.02.50 whilst carrying out a practice attack, the pilot allowed the aircraft to descent too low and it struck the sea and disitegrated. Pilot III **Lewis V. FIRMIN** was killed. SOC.

PK717
33 MU 11.10.46; Westland 05.04.49 for mods; NEA 14.12.54. Sold for scrap 28.06.56.

PK718
33 MU 09.10.46; Westland 27.03.49 for mods; 2 GCF 09.12.52; NEA 14.12.54. Sold for scrap 02.11.56.

PK719
First flight 06.03.46; 33 MU 09.10.46; FEAF 28.03.50; Maintenance Base FE storage 18.05.50; **80 Sqn** Kai Tak 20.09.50; HKAAF 15.05.52; On 12.06.54, whilst engaged in a practice attack on a ground target, the aircraft pulled up sharply and the engine cut. It picked up but items appeared to fall from the aircraft and it stalled and dived vertically into the sea off Shelter Island Hong Kong. Squadron Leader **Eric J.G. GAUNTLETT** was killed.

PK720
First flight 06.03.46; 33 MU 10.10.46; FEAF 28.03.50; Station HQ Kai Tak 24.05.50; **80 Sqn** 20.07.50; HKAAF 15.05.52; On 16.08.53, the aircraft suffered an engine failure and the pilot ditched just off Runway 31 at Kai Tak. The aircraft somersaulted and settled upside down in shallow water. Flying Officer H.L. MOSE escaped major injuries. SOC 16.08.53.

PK721

First flight 19.02.46; 33 MU 05.11.46; Westland 05.04.49; NEA 14.12.54. Sold for scrap 13.06.56.

PK722

First flight 19.02.46; 33 MU 27.09.46; Westland 08.03.49 for mods; NEA 14.12.54. Sold for scrap 28.06.56.

PK723

First flight 27.02.46; 33 MU 26.11.46; RNAS Renfrew 04.07.49; **80 Sqn** FEAF 15.07.49 ; On 23.08.49, the pilot was making his first flight on a Spitfire F.24 and his first sortie from Kai Tak. Despite being briefed to make a dummy approach, overshoot and land from the second, the pilot attempted to land off the first approach but was out of position and tightened his final turn to regain the runway heading. The aircraft stalled at low height and dived into the ground. Flying Officer **William R. PICKERING** killed. SOC.

PK724

First flight 27.02.46; 33 MU 30.10.46; Westland 01.04.49 for mods; NEA 14.12.54; Instructional airframe RAF Brize Norton as 7288M 04.11.55. Extant RAF Museum Hendon.

PK725

First flight 27.02.46; 33 MU 13.09.46; Westland 02.02.49 for mods; NEA 14.12.54. Sold for scrap 28.06.56.

PK726

First flight 06.03.46; 33 MU 05.11.46; Westland 31.03.49 for mods. Originally F.22 but finish as F.24. No further details.

VN301

First flight 14.03.46 as F.22; 33 MU 03.04.46; Vickers-Armstrong 06.05.46 for F.24 conversion; **80 Sqn** 15.01.48. NEA 13.02.54. Sold for scrap 15.05.56.

VN302

First flight 14.03.46; Middle Wallop 19.09.46; CRD Vickers-Armstrong 30.11.46; Vickers-Armstrong High Post Aerodrome 22.01.47 for hand tests with various external stores; CFE 20.04.48. SOC 24.05.54.

VN303

33 MU 10.07.46; **80 Sqn** BAFO 23.02.48; Vickers-Armstrong for repairs 20.07.48 but repairs probably not carried out. NES 13.12.54. Sold for scrap 17.02.56.

VN304

First flight 20.03.46; 33 MU 30.04.46; Vickers-Armstrong for mods 06.05.46; **80 Sqn** BAFO 18.02.48; Vickers-Armstrong 15.10.48; shipped FEAF 02.07.49; Kai Tak 20.09.50. SOC 04.10.50.

VN305

33 MU 12.07.46; **80 Sqn** BAFO 29.09.48; shipped FEAF 02.07.49. On 28.12.49, the pilot was engaged on a cine gun exercice and called to say that his engine had stopped and that he was baling out. However despite a search lasting two days, no trace of the aircraft or pilot were ever recovered. Flying Officer **Kenneth R. ROSEWALL** was killed.

VN306

Vickers-Armstrong 17.04.46; Sent at Kevill 28.09.46 for mods; **80 Sqn** BAFO 16.08.48. On 07.03.49 the aircraft was positioned at No.2 in a formation flying and aerobatic sortie. The formation was pulling out of a shallow dive but the aircraft struck the ground, possibly because the pilot had a red-out which obscured his vision. Pilot III **Ronald A. CLEMENTS** died later from his injuries.

VN307

33 MU 26.04.46; Vickers-Armstrong 06.05.46; **80 Sqn** BAFO 23.02.48; shipped FEAF 02.7.49; damaged in accident 24.01.51; not repaired and SOC 05.07.51.

VN308

33 MU 30.04.46; Vickers-Armstrong 06.05.46; **80 Sqn** 15.01.48; shipped FEAF 02.07.49; Kai Tak 13.12.49; HKAAF 15.05.52. SOC 11.12.53.

VN309

33 MU 30.04.46; Vickers-Armstrong 06.05.46; 1BR&SD BAFO 20.01.49; **80 Sqn** 17.01.49; shipped FEAF 02.07.50. SOC 22.08.51.

VN310

33 MU 26.07.46; **80 Sqn** 15.01.48; shipped FEAF 15.08.49. On 12.01.51, the Spitfire was in formation in cloud with others. It was

Above, Spitfire F.24 VN309, W2-D, taken in flight off Hong Kong. Note the badge painted on the fin, a very close version of the official 80 Sqn's badge and the simplified version painted during the first stages of the usage of the F.24 by the Squadron.

Middle, VN311/W2-C at Lübeck, still wearing the wartime roundels. Because of the absence of any squadron badge on the fin, that leads to think that this photo was probably taken early in 1948. VN311 was among the first F.24s to be allocated to 80 Sqn in January 1948.
(Andrew Thomas)

Below, VN311 was allocated in February 1949, and was wearing the the post-war roundels. Something unusual however, the codes, painted in a shaded style. This seems to have been an oddity within the Squadron. The colours are not determined with certainty, but are believed to be yellow.
(Andrew Thomas)

Two photos of VN318 taken at various moment of its career. Above VN318 taken while being on display in UK before being issued to No.80 Sqn in February 1948. Here, the Spitfire F.24 is showing to the public the ordonnance it can carry, bombs under the left wing and rockets under the right wing. An extra fuel tank is installed under the belly *(Don Hannah - Peter Arnold)*

Bottom,
Issued to No.80 Sqn in February 1948, VN318 was later sent to Hong Kong with the code W2-F, and later transferred to the HKAAF in 1952.

seen to go into a climb and the pilot reported that his instruments had toppled. It seems propable that the aircraft suffered a failure of its pressure instruments because of problems with the suction system. Flight Lieutenant **Denis F. WHITE** killed.

VN311
33 MU 26.07.46; **80 Sqn** 15.01.48; NEA 13.12.54. Sold for scrap 15.05.56.

VN312
33 MU 26.07.46; **80 Sqn** BAFO 09.02.48; shipped FEAF 15.08.49. On 09.06.50, the aircraft was blown into Harvard KF369 by a strong gust of wind whilst taxying at Kai Tak. Not reapaired and SOC 07.07.50.

VN313
First flight 28.02.46; 33 MU 14.08.46; Reserve Pool BAFO 02.05.49; **80 Sqn** 10.06.49; shipped FEAF 02.07.49; HKAAF 15.05.52 On 03.10.53, this aircraft's port wheel went into soft ground and it turned through 180 degrees, lost its undercarriage before striking an accomodation building. Pilot, Pilot Officer George BAIN unhurt. SOC.

VN314
First flight 20.03.46 as a F.22; 33 MU 30.04.46; Vickers-Armstrong 06.05.46 for F.24 conversion; **80 Sqn** BAFO 28.03.49; shipped FEAF 15.08.49. SOC 12.02.51.

VN315
Built as a F.22. A&AEE 09.07.46 Handling trials Sqdn trials 11.06.47; **80 Sqn** 06.02.48; Vickers-Armstrong 12.10.48 for F.24 conversion; **80 Sqn** 06.02.49. NEA 14.12.54; GBEE fitment 10.11.55; Thum Flt Woodvale 24.01.56. NEA 25.05.56. Sold for scrap 30.10.56.

VN316
First flight 02.04.46. Conversion F.24 27.04.46; ECFS 03.05.46; 2 GCF 20.08.51. NEA 13.12.54. Sold for scrap 15.05.56.

VN317
ECFS 18.07.46; 1 BR&SD 01.01.49; **80 Sqn** 12.01.49. On 02.07.49, the Squadron was being redeployed from RAF Gutersloh to RAF Kai Tak and its aircraft were being flown to Renfrew, prior to being loaded onto HMS *Ocean* for transportation to the Far East. The pilot selected the wheels down but did not ensure that the lever was fully home nor did he check for locked down indicator lights. red verey lights were fired too late and the propellers touched the runway. The pilot opened the throttle but the aircraft would not climb away and so he closed the throttle and crashed landed the aircraft, after which it caught fire. The pilot was tired after two long flights and was suffering from the effects of innoculations. Squadron Leader Eric W. TREMLETT safe. SOC 22.07.49.

Only eight of No.80 Sqn's Mk.24 were passed to the HKAAF which used them until 1955. The only external change made to the aircraft was the removal of No.80 Sqn's codes. However it also seems that all flew in an overall silver finish.

VN324 is now good for scrap! Never allocated to a unit, it was however used for various test programms. VN324 is seen at Cosford in 1956.
(Charles Waterfall - Peter Arnold Col.)
Below, another sad view of a line-up of Spitfire F.24s at Cosford waiting for their final fate. In the forefront, VN325 and just behind it, PK713, two airframes which were stored all their career long.

VN318

RAE 7.46; CRD 30.11.46; **80 Sqn** 23.02.48; HKAAF 01.04.52. SOC 21.04.55.

VN319

33 MU 04.07.46; **80 Sqn** 18.02.48. On 28.10.48, this aircraft was leading a formation of Spitfires when it was stuck from below and behind by VN323 in the formation. The pilot who had over 1800 flying hours - including 1300 on Spitfires - attempted to bale out but his parachute opened before he had left the cockpit and he was fatally injured. Squadron Leader **Richard A. NEWBERRY** killed.

VN320

33 MU 29.07.46, **80 Sqn** BAFO 01.03.48. NEA 14.02.54. Sold for scrap 13.06.56.

VN321

First flight 22.07.46; 33 MU 29.07.46. NEA 13.12.54. Sold for scrap 17.02.56.

VN322

First flight 23.07.46; 33 MU 29.07.46; **80 Sqn** BAFO 18.02.48; as scrap 08.09.49. NEA 16.06.53. Sold 19.02.54.

VN323

First flight 23.07.46; 33 MU 29.07.46; **80 Sqn** 09.02.48. Air collision on 28.10.48 with VN319 crash-landed Hombrink Lezze Germany but pilot - Flight Lieutenant Robert W. HALL - bailed out safely (see VN319 for details).

VN324

First flight 13.07.46; CRD 30.11.46; Vickers-Armstrong 16.06.47; GGS for vibration tests AAEE 31.12.47 for full gunnery acceptance trials (Mk.V cannons); Vickers-Armstrong stored until 1950; RAE 12.10.50 on loan Vickers-Armstrong for Lympne air races nea 14.12.54; Sold for scrap 25.06.56.

VN325

First flight 26.07.46; 33 MU 29.07.46; Westland 12.03.49 for mods. NEA 14.12.54. Sold for scrap 31.10.56.

VN326

33 MU 11.11.46; Westland 20.01.49 for mods; shipped FEAF 02.09.50; Maintenance Base FE storage 08.12.50; 390 MU 29.02.53. SOC 18.02.54.

VN327

First flight 06.09.46; 33 MU 21.09.46; Westland for mods 19.01.49. NEA 11.05.56. Sold for scrap 31.10.56.

VN328

First flight 09.09.46; 33 MU 21.09.46; Westland 11.03.49. NES 14.12.54. Sold for scrap 31.10.56.

VN329

First flight 30.09.46; Vickers-Armstrong 11.10.46; AAEE 28.10.46 for full gunnery acceptance trials with Mk.V cannon and comparison trials with PK547 the latter acting as chase plane. Vickers-Armstrong 01.10.47; Westland 06.04.49 for mods. NEA 14.12.54. Sold for scrap 17.02.56.

VN330

First flight 09.10.46; 33 MU 04.11.46; Westland for mods 06.01.49; Shipped FEAF 15.11.50; 390 MU 28.02.53. SOC 18.02.54.

VN331

First flight 19.03.47; Vickers-Armstrong 19.03.47; 9 MU 11.06.47; RNAS Renfrew 29.06.47; Seletar 12.08.49; Station HQ Kai Tak 03.10.50; **80 Sqn** 01.08.51. SOC 01.07.53.

VN332

First flight 25.03.47; 47 MU 28.05.47; Task 322 London Beaverlake to Canada RCAF Winter Estab Edmonton Alberta 24.08.47 cocooning and winterisation trials recocooned Aug-48 dismantled Sep-49. Sold in Canada 21.03.51 reregistered as N7929A.

VN333

6 MU 16.01.47; Vickers-Armstrong for mods and 6 MU 09.03.49 for completion of mods; 33 MU 10.10.51. NEA 13.12.54. Sold for scrap 15.05.56.

VN328 taken in June 1953 at Hatfield. Another airframe never allocated to any unit and stored until being scrapped in 1956. It seems that some stored F.24s found an unexepected utility in being displayed during air shows in UK during the early fifties. Note that VN328 had seen its guns removed.
(Top: JMG Gradidge - Peter Arnold Collection)

Below, Spitfire F.24 VN489/W2-A which became the CO's mount, seen here flying over the colony in 1951. Note the sophisticated squadron badge painted over the fin flash and the white/black fuselage stripes. Left a view from above showing the stripes painted on the wings.
(Andrew Thomas)

VN334

6 MU 16.01.47; Vickers-Armstrong for mods and 6 MU 09.03.49 for completion of mods; 45 MU 19.10.51; Shipped FEAF 29.10.51. NEA 14.12.54. Sold for scrap 31.10.56.

VN477

First flight 12.05.47; 6 MU 07.08.47; Vickers-Armstrong for mods 10.03.49; 45 MU 19.10.51; shipped FEAF 03.11.52. NEA 14.12.51 Sold for scrap 19.06.56.

VN478

First flight 23.06.47; 6 MU 07.08.47; Vickers-Armstrong for mods 09.03.49; 45 MU 17.10.51; shipped FEAF 26.11.52. NEA 11.05.56 Sold for scrap 31.10.56.

VN479

Vickers-Armstrong 06.04.48; 6 MU 30.05.48; shipped FEAF 08.08.48; Maintenance Base FE storage 16.08.48. SOC 18.02.54.

VN480

9 MU 28.08.47; RNAS Renfrew 29.0649; Seletar 12.08.49; **80 Sqn** 27.12.49. SOC 10.12.51.

VN481

Vickers-Armstrong 15.08.48 for investigation of longitude behaviour; 9 MU 03.09.48; RNAS Renfrew 29.06.49; Seletar 12.09.49; Station HQ Kai Tak 14.08.50; **80 Sqn** 05.09.50. SOC 01.09.52.

VN482

9 MU 03.10.47; RNAS Renfrew 29.06.49; Seletar 29.06.49. SOC 15.01.51.

VN483

First flight 23.07.47; 6 MU 07.08.47; Vickers-Armstrong for mods 03.03.48; shipped FEAF 27.03.50. Station HQ Kai Tak 24.05.50; **80 Sqn** 26.07.50; 390 MU 01.03.52. SOC 01.07.53.

VN484

First flight19.06.47; 6 MU 07.08.47; Vickers-Armstrong for mods 28.02.49; shipped FEAF 27.03.50; Maintenance Base FE Kai Tak 14.08.50; **80 Sqn** 27.10.50; 390 MU 01.03.52. SOC 01.07.53.

VN484/W2-H taken in flight in 1949 with basic markings painted on. Note the absence of the badge on the fin, rather unusual for a 80 Squadron's F.24.
(Andrew Thomas)

VN485
First flight 27.08.47; 9 MU 04.09.47; RNAS Renfrew Sep-49; Seletar Station HQ Kai Tak 03.10.50; **80 Sqn** 05.09.51; Hong Kong AAF 13.05.52. Last flight 15.01.55 - FH241.40 - . To 7326M extant Kai Tak 10.04.56.

VN486
First flight 15.07.47; 6 MU 07.08.47; Vickers-Armstrong for mods 03.03.49; Shipped FEAF 27.03.50; **80 Sqn** 24.05.50; 390 MU 01.03.52. SOC 10.02.53.

VN487
First flight 02.09.47; 9 MU 11.09.47; RNAS Renfrew 11.09.47; Seletar 12.08.48; Maintenance Base FE. The aircraft was being used for continuation training and was approaching to land. The pilot allowed it to stall about 60 yards short of the runway. The aircraft stuck the ground in the undershot with its starboard wings, ran into the runway and its undercarriage collapsed. Seletar 07.12.49. SOC.

VN488
First flight 19.09.47. 6 MU 10.10.47; Vickers-Armstrong for mods 28.06.49; **80 Sqn** 15.08.49. SOC 28.08.51.

VN489
First flight 02.10.47; 6 MU 27.10.47; Vickers-Armstrong for mods 09.03.49; RNAS Renfrew 28.06.49; Seletar 12.08.49; **80 Sqn** 27.12.49. SOC 10.12.51.

VN490
First flight 14.11.47; 6 MU 15.12.47; Vickers-Armstrong for mods 17.03.49; RNAS Renfrew 28.06.49; Seletar 12.08.49. SOC 27.11.52.

VN491
First flight 16.10.47; 6 MU 27.10.47; Vickers-Armstrong for mods 10.03.49; RNAS Renfrew 28.06.49; Seletar 12.08.49; **80 Sqn** 27.12.49. On 26.07.50, the aircraft entered a spin from which the pilot did not recover and the aircraft stuck the sea 2m south of Ninepin Is, one of the numerous islands of Hing Kong. Flight Lieutenant **Archibald P. CLARK** killed.

Spitfire F.24 VN492/N of the HKAAF seen on 03.10.53 after it swung while landing at Sek Kong and went off the runway. The port wheel struck a drainage ditch, the starboard undercarriage was damaged and the aircraft tipped up on its nose. The pilot, P/O Rufus Heard escaped injuries.
(G. Cairns)

VN492

First flight 15.12.47; 9 MU 23.12.47; Chilbolton on short term loan CSA charge 15.01.48; RNAS Renfrew 29.06.49; Seletar 12.08.49; Station HQ Kai Tak 03.10.50; **80 Sqn** 01.02.51; HKAAF 15.05.52. On 03.10.43, the aircraft swung off ruwnay to port on landing at Sek Kong and after stricking drainage ditch with the port wheel, tipped onto the nose. Pilot Officer Rufus HEARD unhurt. SOC 19.07.54.

VN493

First flight 24.11.47; 6 MU 11.12.47; RNAS Renfrew 30.06.48; Vickers-Armstrong for mods 04.04.49; **80 Sqn** 15.08.49. SOC 28.08.51.

VN494

First flight 19.12.47; 9 MU 14.01.48; shipped FEAF 22.10.50; Maintenance Base FE storage 26.10.50; Singapore AF 23.07.51. SOC 18.02.54.

VN495

9 MU 21.01.48; RNAS Renfrew 29.06.49; Seletar 12.08.49; **80 Sqn** 05.09.49. SOC 28.08.51.

VN496

First flight 24.02.48 final Spit variant to leave Supermarine production line. Del to 6 MU AAEE 04.04.49; RNAS Renfrew 30.06.49; **80 Sqn** 15.08.49. SOC 15.12.50.

Abbreviations:
CFE: Central Fighter Establishment, CRD: Controller of Research & Development, GCF: Gunnery Co-operation Flight; ECFS: Empire Central Flying School, MU: Maintenance Unit; NEA: Non-effective Airframe; NES: Non-effective Stock; SOC: Struck off Charge

Rather of poor quality but of high interest showing Wing Commander William A. 'Tiny' Nel's aircraft who chose as personal mount VN496. As being the WinCo flying of Kai Tak he was allowed to paint his initials on his aircraft as well the WingCo pennant. The initials are believed to be black. 'Tiny' Neil had been a South African of the Permanent Force who had served in the Desert with No.40 Sqn, SAAF, during the war and had been awarded the DFC and Bar within a period of six months. After the war he transferred to the RAF.
(Andrew Thomas)

Spitfire F.24 VN332 was sent to Canada for winterisation trials. Once completed, VN332 was strcuk off charge and eventually found its way on the civil market in the USA. VN332 is seen here with its American civil registration N7929A in1953 *(Dick Phillips - Peter Arnold Collection)*

✝

ROLL OF HONOUR

SPITFIRE F.24

Name	Rank	Origin	Date	BuNo
CLARK, Archibald Peter	F/L	RAF	26.07.50	VN491
CLEMENTS, Ronald Arthur	P.III	RAF	07.03.49	VN306
FIRMIN, Lewis Victor	P.III	RAF	27.02.50	PK716
GAUNTLETT, Eric John Gerard	S/L	RAF	12.06.54	PK719
NEWBERRY, Richard Alfred	S/L	RAF	28.10.48	VN319
PICKERING, William Rhodes	F/O	RAF	23.08.49	PK723
ROSEWALL, Kenneth Russell	F/O	RAF	28.12.49	VN305
WHITE, Denis Francis	F/L	RAF	12.01.51	VN310

Total: 8

Another view on VN489, the CO's mount, flying over the British Colony and giving in the same time the sensation of power; but the Spitfire F.24 did not had the opportunity to demonstrate its capabilities in combat.
(Peter Arnold Col.)

Supermarine Spitfire F.24 VN311
No. 80 Squadron
Lübeck (Germany), 1948

Supermarine Spitfire F.24 VN317
No. 80 Squadron
Lübeck (Germany), 1948

Supermarine Spitfire F.24 VN489
No.80 Squadron
Squadron Leader Eric W. TREMLETT
Kai Tak (Hong Kong), 1951

Supermarine Spitfire F.24 VN318
No.80 Squadron
Kai Tak (Hong Kong), 1951

Supermarine Spitfire F.24 VN496
Wing Commander William A. 'Tiny' NEL
Kai Tak (Hong Kong), 1950

SQUADRONS!
No.3

The Supermarine SPITFIRE in the...

Fighter Leaders
of the RAF, RAAF, RCAF, RNZAF & SAAF in WW2

Volume I
Phil H. Listemann

Volume III
Phil H. Listemann

USN AIRCRAFT 1922-1962

Vol.4:
Type Designation Letters
'BF', 'BT' & 'F' (Pt-1)

RAF, Dominion & Allied Squadrons at War:
Study, History and Statistics

No.137 Squadron
1941 - 1945

COMPILED BY

PHIL H. LISTEMANN
WITH
CHRIS THOMAS

SQUADRONS!
No.10

The North American
Mustang Mk. IV
in Western Europe

www.RAF-IN-COMBAT.com

- USN Aircraft 1922-1962 -
- Squadrons! -
- RAF, Dominion and Allied squadrons at War -
- Allied Wings -
- Famous squadrons of WW2 -
- Fighter Leaders -

RAF, Dominion & Allied Squadron at War:
Study, History and Statistics

No.131 (County of Kent) Squadron
1941 - 1945

Famous Commonwealth Squadrons of WW2

No.453 (R.A.A.F) Squadron
1941-1945
Buffalo, Spitfire

Phil H. Listemann

ALLIED WINGS

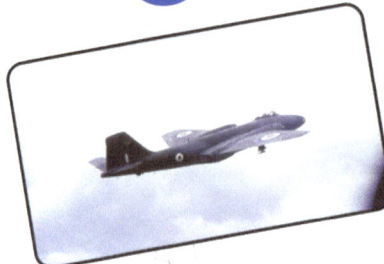

No.19

The English Electric CANBERRA
B(I).8

PHIL H. LISTEMANN

ALLIED WINGS

No.18

The Supermarine SPITFIRE
F.24

PHIL H. LISTEMANN

www.ingramcontent.com/pod-product-compliance
Lightning Source LLC
LaVergne TN
LVHW072116070426
835510LV00002B/78